Seeing God's Design Behind Menopause

Embracing the Powerful Transformational Process

By Vicki Eitel

Cover Photo by David Eitel

Vicki Eitel
Visit my website at www.VickiEitel.com

Printed in the United States of America

First Printing: January 2018
V4 Victorious, LLC

ISBN-9781976930096

I dedicate this book to my sister Anne and my daughter Katherine. May this book make your journey through menopause a little smoother. I give special thanks to my husband David and Lacey Bowcock for believing in me and encouraging me to write this book, and Audrey Loverin, who held my hand every step of the way, and without whom, I would never have accomplished this work.

Contents

Vicki Eitel

Letter From the Author

My Dear Sisters,

You are about to embark upon one of the most amazing journeys of your life. It is the journey of becoming. The voyage is long and often hard, but the land at the end of the journey is worth all the hardships endured. Menopause is a beautiful process designed by God to transform you into the extraordinary woman He created you to be.

The physical, mental and spiritual transformation that takes place in your body during menopause is on a par with the magnitude of changes associated with puberty, and yet almost no one prepares you for the changes that are about to take place. Puberty was God's process to transform you from a little girl into a beautiful woman and mother. Now, with your childbearing years behind you, God now takes you through another transformation and prepares you for the next exciting season of your life. Puberty took approximately 10 years from start to finish. It completely transformed your physical appearance, modified your brain and thought processes, changed your likes and dislikes, wreaked havoc on your emotions, and turned on your ovaries to begin their monthly cycle. As your hormones changed, you underwent the great metamorphosis from child to woman.

Likewise, menopause is a time of metamorphosis. It is a time when your physical appearance changes, your brain rewires, your thought processes alter, your likes and dislikes shift, your emotions go haywire, and your ovaries begin the process of shutting down. All these changes can make for a stormy journey, as it was in puberty, but the very storms are what God uses to strip away all the unnecessary cargo you are carrying and allows you to jettison the parts of yourself you will not need in the next phase of your life.

In the book *The Mermaid Chair* by Sue Monk Kidd, the main character, Jessie, creates a series of paintings of a mermaid diving deeper and deeper into the ocean. As she plunges further and further down, parts of her life are thrown off and float to the surface as she seeks to find the very depths of herself. Menopause forces you to look into the innermost parts of yourself; the very core of who you are and who you want to become. It is a time of discovery. Your soul seems to cry out, "Who am I?" "What do I want to do with my life?" "Who am I becoming?" "What is important to me?" The questions go on and on as you seek to uncover your true self, which is buried inside, waiting to be uncovered and set free.

These stormy waters can be frightening at times, but I want you to know the beauty of the joy set before you. The land at the end of the journey is a land of joy, peace, contentment, confidence, and wisdom; a place where you are free to be yourself and feel comfortable in your own skin. It is a land of new discoveries of hidden talents you didn't know you possessed, of incredible creativity and of renewed purpose and passion.

My desire in this book isn't to give you all the answers or tell you how to avoid hot flashes and other symptoms, but to help you navigate this journey called menopause without the fear and confusion so many women struggle through due to lack of knowledge. God designed your body to go through this process, and though it may be turbulent at times, it shouldn't be fraught with fear and the unknown.

This book is my gift to you. It is not a medical book and is intentionally brief. Most women approaching menopause do not have time to read a 300 page book so I will just be giving you an overview of what to expect. If you want more details, the library has many excellent books on the subject. This is just one women's attempt to pass along some of what I learned and experienced through my own journey. I also want to share with you the hidden design and God-ordained purpose behind menopause. Just as puberty had a grand purpose behind it, menopause does as well. Menopause is a time of great transformation as your body is prepared for the next stage of your life. I look forward to taking this journey with you, bringing understanding and watching you transform into the woman you were destined to be.

Love,

Vicki

Introduction

It was the best of times, it was the worst of times, it was the age of wisdom, it was the age of foolishness, it was the epoch of belief, it was the epoch of incredulity, it was the season of Light, it was the season of Darkness, it was the spring of hope, it was the winter of despair, we had everything before us, we had nothing before us . . .
- Charles Dickens, A Tale of Two Cities

My Story

$\mathcal{I}$ never witnessed my mom going through menopause. She died when she was 49. I was 22. As I entered my thirties and the process of menopause, I was totally in the dark and had no idea what to expect or when to expect it. My journey through the choppy waters of menopause were worse than most. Many women sail through with barely a warm breeze while others feel as though they have survived a category 5 hurricane. Most women experience something in between. As you read my story, and even the rest of this book, realize that your experience will be different and hopefully devoid of many of the symptoms others and I have experienced.

In my late thirties, I was a stay-at-home mom with two elementary age children and happily homeschooling them. I was very active and had always been really healthy. Until one day, out of nowhere, I began experiencing a wide variety of physical ailments that seemed completely unrelated. They began with an onslaught of migraines two to five days a week. I was sent to a neurologist who ordered a CAT scan. "Everything looks fine," the doctor said. "Some women just seem to start getting migraines as they get older." He suggested keeping a food log to see if there were any foods triggering them. This answer wasn't very satisfactory. Why were foods that I had always eaten suddenly causing me migraines? He didn't have an answer.

Then one day during Vacation Bible School, I jumped up to grab a piece of tape off the ceiling and when I landed my heart started racing like I had just run the 200 meter sprint. Should I call 911? Was I having a heart attack? After two or three minutes, my heart went back to beating normally. As the weeks went by, it didn't race again but started skipping beats. I went to the doctor and was referred to a cardiologist who ran a stress test, injected dye to take an image of my heart, and had me wear a monitor for two weeks during which time I was to press a button every time I felt my heart skip a beat. The final verdict, "Everything looks fine. As some women grow older, it just seems to happen." Again, not a very satisfactory answer.

From that point on, my health began to take a turn for the worse. What was happening to me? The most alarming aspect wasn't the problems themselves but the sheer number of problems. Not only was I experiencing migraines and heart irregularities, but my energy level seemed to be getting lower and lower, and my digestive tract began to go crazy with bloating, burning, and constipation. I also began having pain in my joints, swelling, weight gain, low sex drive and there seemed to be something wrong with my brain. It was as if my brain was in a fog most of the time and making the simplest of decisions became a major undertaking. And the fatigue—I didn't seem to be able to do much of anything. I had to force my way through each day. I would sleep in the car during my children's music lessons and want to cry when it was time to open my eyes and drive them home.

A fear began to creep into my mind. Was I dying? Did I have cancer, lupus or fibromyalgia? I was referred to many different specialists and had numerous tests run, but always the same diagnosis. "Everything looks fine." No matter how many times I heard this pronouncement, I knew I wasn't fine. Something was wrong with me.

After doing some research on my own, I finally came to the conclusion that I was suffering from perimenopause. I suggested this diagnosis to my gynecologist only to have her angrily respond, "You are too young to be going through menopause and there is no such thing as perimenopause. Besides, perimenopause simply means "before menses stops. So technically, you have been going through perimenopause since the day you started your period." Six months later, my period stopped. I had indeed been going through early menopause.

The medical community has come a long way over the last 15 years in recognizing the symptoms and changes associated with perimenopause. At the time I was going through it, most doctors staunchly denied any such thing as perimenopause, and the word itself was fairly new. Now there is a wealth of books on the subject, and doctors are educated on the symptoms and treatment of perimenopause. Although there are now many resources on perimenopause available, most women have no clue the symptoms they are experiencing are related to their changing hormones. This ignorance causes a great deal of fear and frustration and even a certain amount of self-condemnation, as they seem to be unable to focus and do the things they used to do.

As I began to realize that I was going through early menopause, I became upset with the women in my life who had failed to prepare me and teach me what to expect. I was struck by the difference in how we approach preparing our daughters for menses versus preparing our daughters for menopause.

When our daughters begin to approach the age of puberty we watch them closely for the first signs of "the change." We notice when the breast buds begin to form and hair begins to show up in new places. We go to great pains to talk to them and teach them about what to expect. The schools even hold special assemblies for girls and boys to talk about the changes that are going to happen to their bodies.

When my daughter was ten, I began to share with her how her body would begin to change. When she turned eleven, I took her away for the weekend for a mother and daughter retreat. I made her a basket filled with tampons, pads, deodorant, razors, a pretty shirt, some earrings and other fun items. The basket included a book on the birds and the bees and another book on growing up. I showed her how to use the feminine hygiene products and discussed the menstrual cycle, mood swings, and sexuality.

I walked by her side as her body changed, answering questions and showing her how to care for her body. As her skin became oilier, I taught her about skin care. When the hair on her legs became dark and the hair under her arms came in, I showed her how to shave. As soon as her breasts began to appear I took her shopping for her first bra. When she burst into tears and had no idea why she was crying, I held her and helped her understand how hormones can affect our moods. The day she started her period, I was right there, helping her along.

Most of us would think it was terrible if the only thing a girl was told prior to going through puberty was that one day she would start bleeding when there are so many other areas of her body is being effected from breasts, to skin, to body odors, to brain development. And yet, this is exactly how society treats women who are approaching menopause. All we are told is that our periods will stop and we'll have hot flashes. We, as a society, have dropped the ball in passing along the information women need to know about how their bodies will change, how to respond to those changes, and how to take care of themselves.

My desire with this book is to ease the transition for other women and alleviate some of the fear and frustration I, and many of my friends, experienced due to lack of information and being woefully unprepared. In the following pages, I want to take every woman in her late thirties on a mother-daughter retreat and prepare her for the days ahead. I want to give her a basket filled with the items she will need to navigate the changes that take place as she journeys into the next stage of life. I would also love to see mothers use this book as a spring board to prepare their own daughters for what lies ahead and open the door of communication. It's time for women to cease being silent on this subject and share the information we've learned and experiences we've had with one another, to prepare those who come behind us or journey alongside us.

Part 1
What's Happening to Me?

Chapter 1
Changes to the Body

What Is Menopause?

M enopause is the period right before and right after menstruation stops, marking the end of reproduction. The term menopause can be confusing because it is used in many different ways to mean different things. It technically means the point in time when menstruation stops. The medical community will declare you have reached menopause when you have gone one year without a period. However, the term menopause is also used to describe the changes the body is going through in the years before and after menopause. In an effort to alleviate some of the confusion, the term perimenopause was coined. Perimenopause is used to describe the changes occurring before (peri) menstruation stops and the term post-menopause for the years after menstruation stops. There is no standard usage. In this book, I use menopause to describe the whole process, perimenopause through post-menopause and only use perimenopause when specifically talking about the period of time before menstruation stops.

Symptoms

*"I wonder if there's any point in going on," said
Susan. "I mean. It doesn't seem particularly safe
here and it looks as if it won't be much fun either."*
- C.S. Lewis, The Lion the Witch and the Wardrobe

Each woman is born with a finite number of eggs. The ovaries produce estrogen and progesterone and control menstruation and ovulation. When the ovaries stop releasing eggs, menstruation stops. Most women go through menopause after the age of 40. Perimenopause begins several years before menstruation stops as the production of estrogen begins to decrease. During the last 1 or 2 years before menopause, the drop in estrogen quickens and many women begin to experience menopause symptoms.

Perimenopause (and into menopause) is a time when your body is being completely rewired and reconfigured as your ovaries shut down and along with them, the production of estrogen and progesterone. These changing levels of hormones then in turn begin to affect other hormones. As your body seeks new production sites for estrogen, every part of who you are gets affected: body, mind and spirit. This book looks at each of these areas and discusses what to expect during this season of menopause.

The changes occurring during the transition of menopause is of equal magnitude as the changes experienced during puberty. The complete transition of puberty lasts from about age ten through age 20 and likewise, menopause takes about ten years to complete. And just as changes to your body began several years before your period actually started and then continued changing for several years afterwards, so too, changes will begin to take place several years before your period stops and continue on for several years afterwards.

I think the thing that catches most women off guard is that symptoms begin while their periods are still occurring like clockwork. Most of us have the mistaken idea that our periods stop and then we start getting hot flashes (we have no idea that there are any other symptoms to even expect). This misconception is what causes so much fear and anxiety when our bodies begin to go haywire for no apparent reason. The symptoms are so wide and varied and many seem completely unrelated to menopause but are in fact triggered by dropping levels of estrogen. Pamela Smith says in *When Hormones Go Haywire*, "Many women don't make the connection to perimenopause and so they suffer in silence, blame it on stress or move from one specialist to another looking for cures."

Here is a composite list from many different sources on what symptoms you might expect. Though the list can be daunting, few women experience all of these symptoms and some experience hardly any.

CHANGES TO YOUR BODY
- Hot Flashes
- Irregular periods(shorter, longer, heavier, or lighter)
- Increased PMS Symptoms (bloating, cramps, breast tenderness)
- Fatigue
- Skin
  - Dry Skin
  - Sagging Skin/Wrinkles
  - Sticky Skin
- Brittle Nails
- Vaginal Dryness
- Loss of Libido
- Hair

- o Hair Loss
- o Hair Texture Changes
- o Hair Color (dull, graying)
- Sleeping Disorders/Insomnia
- Night Sweats
- Brain
  - o Dizziness
  - o Memory Lapses
  - o Fuzzy Thinking/Difficulty Concentrating
- Weight Gain (especially around the middle)
- Cravings for Sweets and Carbs
- Digestion
  - o Incontinence
  - o Bloating
  - o Heartburn
  - o Acid Reflux
  - o Constipation
  - o Gas/Burping
  - o Irritable Bowel Syndrome
- Allergies
- Body Odor
- Irregular Heartbeat
- Emotions
  - o Mood Swings
  - o Irritability
  - o Depression
  - o Anxiety
  - o Panic Disorder
- Loss of Calcium/Osteoporosis

ACHES AND PAINS
- Headaches / Migraines

- Breast Pain
- Cystitis
- Joint Pain
- Muscle Tension
- Electric Shocks
- Tingling Extremities
- Itchy Skin
- Burning Tongue
- Gum Problems

Are you excited now? Just teasing. No matter how few or how many symptoms you experience, you should always tell your doctor and have your symptoms evaluated. Many of these symptoms are also associated with ailments that are more serious. For example, heart fluctuations and fatigue can be signs of a low thyroid, so be sure to have all your symptoms checked by your doctor.

Remember that mother-daughter retreat I talked about? Here are a few of the things I want you to know about how your body will be changing and what to expect. Though I won't be touching on them all, these are the ones I wish someone had told me about.

Changes in Menstruation

Many women have the misconception that menopause just magically happens one month. They think they will be rolling along, having their monthly cycle and then one month it will stop. This is far from reality. Women experience a variety of changes to their menstrual cycle years before it finally stops. Some women experience changes in frequency. Their periods get closer together or farther apart. The frequency can also change from one month to another. They may have their period every 14 days for three months, stop for 9 months, have some spotting and then start back up again like clockwork coming every 28 days. Other women report changes in the consistency of their periods, either getting thicker or thinner or even stringy. Periods may change color from light brown to dark or bright red. The duration of your period can increase or decrease and the amount of blood flow can become lighter or heavier. The only thing you can know for sure is it will be different for everyone. That is why it is important to get regular check-ups with your gynecologist to make sure there are no underlying problems causing the changes. Once you have gone 365 days without a period, you are usually considered to be in menopause though there is no guarantee that you will never have another one. I think it was three years before I really believed that I was done and felt confident in giving away all my feminine hygiene products.

Hot Flashes

Though hot flashes seem to be the symptom most women want to know about, I am not going to say much here because there is a plethora of information out there, and new treatments come out frequently to help with hot flashes. This a great topic to explore with others, and even research on the internet for the latest trends in research and relief. So talk to other women who are going through menopause and see what they suggest. I will share with you that certain foods can increase the number of hot flashes you have. Unfortunately, the hot flash doesn't always start immediately after the consumption of the food so it will take a little detective work on your part to figure out what triggers them in you. Some of the more well-known triggers are caffeine, spicy foods, and hot liquids (drinks or soups). Drinking lots of water will help, and if you can drink a glass of ice water when you feel a hot flash starting, many times this will stop it in its tracks. I also found this piece of research interesting. It said that prayer and relaxation relieved hot flashes in about 90% of women with no other therapy. How's that for an opportunity to turn a frustration into a positive action? If you experience a hot flash, use it as a reminder to stop and pray, thanking God for his marvelous design of the human body. Meditate for a moment on his power and presence—and ask for a calming breeze of peace to cool your raging body.

Skin and Hair

Wrinkles should merely indicate where smiles have been.
– Mark Twain
The grey head is a crown of glory.
– Proverbs 16:3a

Do you remember going through puberty and learning that you needed to start using special facial soap, shampoo for oily hair, acne cream and deodorant? All of this seemed so foreign and it took time to adjust and learn this new beauty routine. By the same token, as we age and go through menopause, our skin and hair will undergo a similar transition only in reverse. Instead of our skin and hair becoming oilier, it becomes dryer and more brittle. Estrogen is what keeps our skin and hair well-nourished and moisturized. As estrogen decreases, they begin to lose their strength and elasticity and grow thinner. As the skin becomes drier, you may experience itchiness and need to add body lotion to your regime. Skin and hair care products you have used for years, will suddenly appear to stop working, especially if you are using products designed for oily skin. You will find you need to switch moisturizers, shampoos, foundation, and cleansers to products designed to combat aging and dryness.

Now I need to warn you about the following phenomenon. In the beginning, as your skin becomes dryer, wrinkles will slowly begin to appear and be only slightly noticeable. Then one morning, you will wake up, look in the mirror, and **poof** there is a middle-aged woman staring back at you. Where did she come from and what has she done with your face? Most women assume that aging happens in a very gradual process but this doesn't always seem to be the case. Many women I have talked to have reported this overnight aging phenomenon, so be prepared.

For those of you with oily skin, you will be grateful for the reduction in oil production (remember those treasures I said you would receive), but beware; the moisturizers and other skin care products you use for oil control will begin to exacerbate the problem when it comes to wrinkles. As you begin to notice the decrease in greasiness, begin switching to products for normal to dry skin. You might want to consider adding sunscreen to your daily regime as well. It will help prevent age spots.

Your skin is not the only thing changing; your hair also undergoes significant changes. It will begin to lose its sheen, and the color will begin to dull and turn gray. According to my hairdresser, Tammy, anytime we experience changes in our hormones, our hair will be affected. It may become straighter or curlier, lose body or gain body, or become thicker or thinner. The only thing for sure, is that it will change. For me, the changes were great. The added body has allowed me to experiment with new styles and the decrease in oil means I can go two or three days between washings. This was a luxury for this girl, who had to wash it absolutely every day for 30 some years (that's 10,950 shampoos and blow-dries!). I love the time savings!

There are other things to get used to as well. One morning I looked in the mirror and wondered, "What happened to my eyebrows?" They had become so faint I could barely see them. My usually black eyebrows had lightened to the point of being almost imperceptible. Then I looked closer and found my eyebrows had relocated to just above my upper lip. Yikes! An American Psychological Association article called "What Nurses Know About Menopause," states:

> We expect our hair to get gray as we get older. However, many women are not prepared for other hair changes that menopause may bring. As estrogen levels decline, the ratio between estrogen and androgen shifts. Some women find they have more hair on their face and less hair on their head.

So as the aging process moves along, you may need to add some new tools and makeup to your beauty routine: eyebrow pencils, lip pencils and electric facial shavers.

My step-mother, Marilyn, once told me that as women age everything begins to move south and it certainly seems that way. Chins, breasts, hips, and knees all seem to be on a downward slide. But I have found that with all these changes, we must learn to love ourselves in a deeper way. In some strange way, the physical changes of aging bring a freedom from self-consciousness and a new level of self-acceptance. When I was younger, I worried about my looks, and would never go out without my makeup on, but as I have aged, I have found the freedom to go out just as I am. I no longer feel the need to impress anyone, nor do I worry about what people will think. When discussing how our motivation for wearing makeup has changed through menopause, my friend Lacey described it as going from hiding to highlighting. She said we now have permission to bow out of the competition. Instead of feeling like we weren't pretty enough and had to use makeup to make ourselves more beautiful, we now feel beautiful just as we are and use makeup as a way to highlight that beauty. A new sense of self-confidence and contentment seems to permeate our lives.

Beauty

Beauty begins the moment you decide to be yourself.
— Coco Chanel

With all the physical changes of menopause, we often begin to feel old and unattractive. We focus on the wrinkles, the increased weight, the sagging skin, the brown spots and gray hairs. But what defines beauty? I remember one day when I was feeling sorry for myself and feeling less than beautiful, the Lord asked me if I thought all women over the age of fifty were unattractive because they had wrinkles and gray hair. How about you? As I considered the women who were older than me, I realized how beautiful they were, not in the way of youthful beauty, but with a radiance that comes with age. These women radiate peace, joy, and contentment that cannot be found in the young. They were women who were comfortable with themselves and thus made others feel at ease.

Their beautiful white hair seemed to glow like a halo around their heads.

So how do we go about defining beauty? Over the centuries people have tried to define beauty, but what is beautiful to one person isn't necessarily beautiful to another person. Close your eyes for a moment and think about the most beautiful place on earth you have ever seen, the place that most took your breath away. Now, recall the feeling the place invoked. Try and put a name to the different emotions you're feeling. How are those emotions affecting you? I would like to suggest that in the end, beauty is a response, a feeling that is invoked when you gaze upon something that touches you deeply. It is somehow expansive – it expands you on the inside in a way that is hard to describe. You feel full, nourished somehow. You encounter peace, well-being, love, awe, and oneness with our creator. It invites you to linger, to find rest for your soul. It inspires you.

God created women to be carriers of this beauty, this ability to invite, to nourish, to expand, to inspire and offer comfort and rest. God fashioned us to be beauty bearers, to carry beauty everywhere we go, so that when people encounter us or come into our sphere, they encounter peace, acceptance, and nourishment. They want to linger. Have you ever met that kind of woman? The person who always makes you feel refreshed, encouraged, stronger, nourished? My friend Joanie is one of those women. Every time I am with her I want to linger and when I leave, I always feel refreshed. This is what we were created for, to be God's image-bearers, for people to get a taste of the beauty, love, and care of our heavenly Father. We are to nurture the world and guide its people to the creator. When a child falls down and hurts themselves, it runs to its mother. It is in her arms it finds the love, care, and reassurance—peace if you will—that all will be right with the world again. The child finds the strength and refreshment to get back on the bike again, climb the monkey bars, or get back on the horse.

Often, when the story of creation is read, it is read in such a way as to imply that women were somehow an after-thought; created simply to fill in a gap—to be Adam's helper—not having significance of her own, but only as an assistant to Adam. But if you look closely at the story of creation, you will see that with each passing day, with each new creation, God's creations become more and more complex, more sophisticated, and more beautiful. Nature is not primarily functional. Its primary purpose is to display beauty. Think about it, the functional purpose of a tree is to process carbon monoxide into oxygen. So couldn't God have created just one tree or maybe two or three for the different climates and been done with it? Did he have to create thousands of specifies with different barks, different leaves, different colors, with leaves that change in the fall, and some to stay green year-round. Doesn't this variety point to God's primary intent being beauty? If in each stage of creation, God is creating more and more beauty, then the crescendo, the pinnacle of all creation is Eve. She was never an after-thought, but always an integral part of the plan. She was meant to be the crowning achievement of all creation.

You are the crown of all creation.

You are the most beautiful of all creation.

Yes, you!

Ours is a grand purpose, unlike any other creation in all creation. All of creation speaks to different aspects of God's nature. Women were created to display God's beauty, made from His nurturing, relational and life-giving nature. The scripture says, that God said, "It is not good that the man should be alone." Isn't that the truth? How many of you had to read *Lord of the Flies* in high school? As this story illustrates, if a group of boys or men are left to themselves without the presence of a woman, they will end up killing each other. Without the balancing force of women, the world would quickly degenerate into chaos. God knew when he designed Adam; he would have to design an Eve. She wasn't an after-thought, but a divinely planned creation to bring balance and beauty to the world.

Most biblical translations define the Hebrew words *ezer kenegdo* to helper or help-meet. Some translate it as companion. Again, all giving the connotation of an add-on, an adjunct, an assistant. However, the interesting thing about the Hebrew language is its precision. Each time a word is used in scripture, it defines how it will be used in the rest of scripture. Some words are only used to describe God and are never used to describe humans. They are set aside for Him only. Now the fascinating thing about this word *ezer* is that it is exclusively used to describe God except in one place: here in Genesis, to describe Eve. When it is used to describe God as in, "God is my helper (ezer)" and "I cried out to God for help (ezer)", the connotation is a life or death situation. God as my ezer is my life saver, my sustenance, without whom I can't make it, apart from whom I'll die. This describes the purpose for which God created Eve, to be Adam's lifesaver, his counterpart without whom he couldn't live. Women were created in the image of God, in a way that Adam was not. She was to display God's beauty, His majesty, His life giving, life-sustaining, character.

Oh, yes, ladies, we were created with a divine purpose that only we can fulfill. But sadly, many of us have lost our purpose. I watched a clip of the women's march back in February, 2016. My heart wept as woman after woman got on the stage and said, "I'm a nasty woman"—the anger, the hatred, the hardness. This is not what we were created for. We have lost our divine purpose. Think about the two women in the Sound of Music. On the one side you have the stunningly beautiful Baroness and on the other, the cute but rather plain Maria. They are a perfect example of what the world defines as beauty in a woman versus how God defines beauty.

Captain von Trapp is captivated initially by the Baroness's physical beauty and barely takes any notice of Maria. But as the movie progresses, we begin to see that the Baroness, though beautiful, witty and accomplished, is hard and calculating. Maria, on the other hand, sees beauty everywhere, in whiskers on kittens, warm woolen mittens and unruly children. Maria's inner beauty slowly begins to nourish the love-starved Von Trapp children. In her presence, they find hope, inspiration, joy and peace. When they are scared of the storm, they find comfort and safety. As time goes on, her presence begins to reach even the Captain. He finds himself wanting to linger in her presence. The Baroness won his admiration but Maria wins his heart. Where the Baroness filled an empty space in his life, she was not able to bring him healing from the death of his wife. Maria, in contrast, is slowly bringing love, joy and music back into his life. In a sense, she is restoring beauty to his life. She is his *ezer kenegdo*, his lifesaver.

Beauty shines from the inside out. If we will cooperate with the refining fires of menopause and allow God to heal our inner woundedness, He will restore our true beauty. At a class I was giving on menopause, we were discussing the changes to our looks and one woman who had known me for a long time said, "Vicki, I hope you don't mind me saying this, but you are much more beautiful now than you used to be." I knew she was right. I could see it for myself every day in the mirror. When I was younger I hated myself, and thought I was the ugliest person around and in many ways, I was ugly—ugly on the inside. That ugliness showed up on my face and in my countenance. Through the season of menopause, I was forced to look inside myself and work through all the self-hate and self-rejection. I allowed myself to go through the transformation for which Christ died for me. As I began to accept myself and love myself, my outward appearance began to transform. Stasi Eldredge says in Captivating,

Most women doubt very much that they have any genuine beauty to unveil. It is, in fact, our deepest doubt. When it comes to the issues surrounding beauty, we vacillate between striving and resignation. New diets, new outfits, new hair color. Work out; work on your life; try this discipline or that new program for self-improvement. Oh, forget it. Who cares anyway? Put up a shield and get on with life. Hide. Hide in busyness; hide in church activities; hide in depression. There is nothing captivating about me. Certainly not inside me. I'll be lucky to pull it off on the outside. Whatever else it means to be feminine, it is depth and mystery and complexity, with beauty as its very essence. Now, lest despair set in, let us say as clearly as we can: Every woman has a beauty to unveil.

Every woman.

Because she bears the image of God. She doesn't have to conjure it, go get if from a salon, have plastic surgery or breast implants. No, beauty is an essence that is given to every woman at her creation.

You are beautiful.

Cameron Diaz in discussing her book *Longevity* on one of the morning shows said "research shows that people who embrace aging and accept themselves the way they are add six years to their lives and shorten the menopause process." The beautiful women we know have learned this lesson. They are comfortable with themselves and exude love, joy, peace, and contentment and it shows in their countenance. One of the greatest treasures of this journey of menopause is its ability to force us to examine ourselves and unveil our beauty by transforming us into the beautiful women we truly are. The world desperately needs our beauty.

A Time for Reflection

- Are you more like the Baroness or Maria?
- Meditate on the beauty you were meant to carry and offer to the world; beauty that is powerful, inviting, nourishing, comforting, inspiring and causes people to want to linger.
- How can you be a more inviting person people want to linger around?
- How can you nourish those you are speaking to?
- How can you inspire them and release the beauty inside them?

Weight Gain

When our ovaries begin to shut down, the amount of estrogen they produce diminishes greatly and our bodies begin to look for new sources of estrogen to balance out this decrease. Interestingly enough, it turns out that fat cells can produce estrogen and so your body goes on a mission to increase your fat cells and convert your estrogen-manufacturing site from your ovaries to your fat cells. And guess which fat cells are the most effective producers of estrogen? Abdominal cells! This explains why even women who have never struggled with weight gain or had a tummy before, suddenly begin to gain weight around their middle during perimenopause and can't seem to get it off. Your body is trying to add fat cells to your abdomen in order to get the estrogen it needs. Your weight gain is not necessarily a product of what you are eating, your lack of exercise, or your mid-life metabolic slowdown, though those do play a part. Without these few extra pounds, you won't have the necessary supply of estrogen and your symptoms will be greatly exaggerated. So allow a little extra weight—10 to 15 pounds—and enjoy an easier transition. However, be careful, that 10–15 pounds can quickly turn into 30 or 40! Believe me, I know!

As we bemoan this weight gain, it's important to keep our changing bodies in perspective. I read in a book that as women go through menopause their bodies soften all over. It's part of God's design. The softness brings a sense of comfort to those we embrace. As I read, I was reminded of the incredible feeling of being hugged by my grandmother. There was nowhere in the world that felt more secure and comforting than in her soft embrace. It differed from the hard, firm embrace of my mother. One time when I was talking about losing weight, my daughter rather sadly said, "But mom, you are so huggable." Though I had never discussed this particular insight with her, she was affirming the truth of it.

Sex Life

It's late at night, you have worked all day dealing with the kids, running errands, cooking dinner, paying bills. You crawl in bed drained and your husband gives you the signal. Ugh. Not only are you exhausted, but lovemaking has become downright painful.

The decrease in estrogen levels causes a reduction in vaginal moisture, which can make intercourse very painful. So what is a woman to do? There are a number of options. Have more frequent sex—the more sex, the better the lubrication. Yeah, right. If that isn't going to happen anytime soon or you still need more lubrication, you can take estrogen either orally or vaginally, insert a moisturizing suppository into the vagina several times a week, or use a personal lubricant. Which is best? It depends on your bank account, convenience, and how you feel about taking hormones. Talk to your gynecologist about which options might be best for you. For me, a personal lubricant was the easiest.

Several women have asked me, "How do you use a personal lubricant?" The lubricant can be purchased at any drugstore in the aisle where the personal intimacy items are sold. The lubricant comes in the form of a liquid or gel. When the preliminaries of lovemaking are over, squirt some lubricant into your hand and apply it to your husband. Believe me; he will not mind this in the least!

I should add at this point that your sex drive will be very up and down as your hormones fluctuate. Hang in there, your hormones will eventually level out and your sex drive will return. One of the older women in my life once shared with me that one of the best things about becoming an empty nester was the return of your sex life. No longer will you be exhausted from all your responsibilities, nor will you have to worry about being heard or interrupted. You can actually have sex earlicr in the evening when you still have energy rather than waiting until late at night after everyone is in bed. You can even have an afternoon delight if you want. Imagine that!

So, you have that to look forward to....

Changes in Hearing

"Turn that music down!" How many of you remember your mothers telling you to turn down the music or the TV or perhaps just a general, "Will you kids hold it down." One of the more obscure menopausal symptoms some woman experience is sensitivity to sound. Sounds that didn't seem to bother you before now make you feel like someone is running fingernails down a chalkboard.

But hang in there, it is usually only temporary and will subside after you get through menopause. After that, you will start going deaf—just saying!!! Seriously, though, about one-third of all women over 65 experience some hearing loss.

Fatigue and Sleeplessness

I think one of the hardest aspects of menopause to deal with is fatigue. I remember waking up after 9 hours of sleep and feeling so tired I wasn't sure I could get out of bed. All I wanted to do was pull the covers over my head and go back to sleep. What frustrated me the most was having no idea why I was so tired all the time. It turned out to be just one more side effect of my changing hormones. If you find yourself struggling with fatigue, be sure to check with your doctor to rule out anything more serious. Fatigue can also be caused by hypothyroidism, auto-immune diseases, sleeplessness, or lack of exercise.

Your body is going through an incredible change just like it did during puberty and pregnancy. Your body is working overtime making all the changes this season requires. You can get angry at your body and energy level or you can show yourself a little kindness and understanding. When a small child gets cranky in the early afternoon, we smile and say, "Someone needs a nap." We recognize the child's need for sleep and more importantly, we let them sleep. Allowing yourself a nap in the afternoon can do wonders to rejuvenate you. Or, go to bed an hour earlier. All those chores can wait.

Another aspect of fatigue and one of the most debilitating side effects of the changing hormones of menopause is insomnia. The lack of ovulation results in a vast decrease in progesterone. Add to that the increased levels of the stress hormone cortisol and you are in for a long night of staring at the clock. We have all experienced a night or two of insomnia, but when the sleepless nights continue night after night, the mental and physical toll can be tremendous and dangerous. According to Psychology Today, "The first signs of sleep deprivation are unpleasant feelings of fatigue, irritability, and difficulties concentrating. Then come problems with reading and speaking clearly, poor judgment, lower body temperature, and a considerable increase in appetite. If the deprivation continues, the worsening effects include disorientation, visual misperceptions, apathy, severe lethargy, and social withdrawal."

If left untreated, insomnia can lead to heart disease, diabetes, depression, hypertension, obesity, and decreased immune function. If you begin to experience sleeplessness, don't ignore it. Sometimes it can be for just a night or two, but when it begins to go on for more than a few days; it's time to take action. There are many different causes for insomnia so the solution can be as simple as taking a little melatonin to getting a prescription for sleeping pills or progesterone cream. Talk to your doctor and find out what's right for you.

Question: Are you getting enough sleep?

Chapter 2
Changes to the Brain

G od's design of the human body is truly astounding. The more I studied about menopause when I was going through it, the more incredulous I became at the multi-faceted changes built into the process. One of the most fascinating facets was the changes taking place in our brains. Doctors describe them as a literal rewiring that takes place beginning in our 40's. These changes are designed to prepare us for the changes we will experience in our "second adulthood." Holly Shut, in *Midlife Momentum*, describes the second adulthood this way: "Your first adulthood, 25-50 is about establishing a career, building a family, becoming part of a community. This "second adulthood" will look very different from your first. When we realize that at 50 we could very likely live another 30/40+ years we need to explore what we want to be doing with those years." Our brains know that the old systems and ways of thinking will not work for us as we face changing relationships, shifting roles, and new responsibilities. God uses menopause and the changes to our brains to fashion us for the next season of life, a life of purpose which will bring us joy and meaning.

It is interesting to note that the changes taking place in a women's brain during menopause parallel the changes that occur in a male fetus during the 6th week of development. When a fetus is 6 weeks old, a hormone is released that severs the majority of connections between the two sides of the brain. If it is a female fetus, the hormone is not released and all the connections stay intact. This is why women are able to multitask and men tend to focus on one thing at a time. God, in His infinite wisdom, designed women to be able to multitask knowing we would have to be able to watch multiple children, cook, clean, change diapers, and talk on the phone all at the same time. Men, on the other hand, were designed to be hunters and gathers and needed to focus their attention on tracking their prey.

However, as women age, our need for multitasking decreases as our responsibilities at home decrease. God graciously designed our brains to go through pruning and rewiring to give us better efficiency and serve us more effectively in this next stage of life. So He designed our bodies to release a hormone to prune our brains and the connections between the two sides of the brain. This is why older women are characterized as being calmer and more focused than their younger counterparts who are always going in a million directions at once.

This pruning process forces us to re-evaluate and reprioritize what's important to us and where we want to spend our time and energy. What are you passionate about? What is most important? What can you let go of? If we aren't aware of what is taking place in our brains, the process can be very disconcerting. We don't understand why we can no longer juggle the multiple responsibilities that we have always handled with such ease. Feelings of being over-whelmed, out-of-control, and inadequate begin to assail us.

If I could share one word of advice to my younger counterparts, it would be to evaluate where you are spending your time and energy and cut back if you are feeling overwhelmed. When you had small babies and people asked you if you could help with this or that, you had the obvious excuse to say, "No, I can't right now," and you were right. Your energy and time were already spoken for and there was no room to add more to your plate. But during the years of menopause, there is no outwardly visible reason why you should say no, so many of us feel guilty demurring. You need to remember your body and brain are using up tremendous amounts of energy reconfiguring your body. If you are in a season where you are feeling anxious and overwhelmed, give yourself permission to cut back on a few of your lower priority responsibilities. Give your body the rest and space it needs. If you don't, your stress levels will increase dramatically and along with it, ailments of every kind, and in many cases depression and anxiety attacks. Take it from a woman who did it the wrong way. Give yourself the grace to take it easy during these years. You have given your time and energy for many years and will do so again when your hormones level out again, but for now, in this season, save your meager reserves for the commitments most important to you. Your body will thank you.

Memory Loss

"Honey, what are you laughing about?"

"That scene from the movie last week."

"What movie?"

"The one we watched last weekend."

(Blank stare)

"You've Got Mail."

"You've Got Mail?" (No memory of seeing that movie)

"What was it about?"

"You know, about the girl who meets a guy online and they start communicating through email and eventually fall in love."

I continue to stare blankly at my husband. He proceeds to recount the entire movie, and I still have absolutely no memory of it. We stare at each other in disbelief. But I have no memory of the movie. This wasn't the first time in the last year or two when I seemed to have amnesia. There were lost conversations, lost outings and a variety of other small episodes. I had begun to worry that I had a brain tumor or some other dreaded disease. How could I possibly forget an entire movie I watched just one week ago? To say I was getting scared was an understatement. With all the other physical problems I was experiencing, fear was becoming a constant companion. It didn't help that all the doctors kept telling me I was fine and there was nothing wrong with me. Hello, I just forgot an entire movie! What do you mean there is nothing wrong with me?

Lapses in memory can be very disconcerting but they are often caused by the pruning activity being conducted on your brain. You can lose bits of information or yes, entire movies. After finally discovering the cause of my amnesia, I was able to laugh about my memory lapses. When my husband would ask me about something and I couldn't remember saying or doing it, I would just laugh and say, that must have gotten snipped, please remind me what I said/did. I used to argue with him that he never told me that or I never said/did that, but now I was able to give him the benefit of the doubt and realize that he was probably right. Post-it© notes became my constant companion. I kept a pack of notes in every room of the house. If I thought of something I needed to do, I would write it down and then carry the note with me until I did it, or I would stick it on the kitchen counter where I kept my "memory." My counter looked like a patchwork quilt with all the different notes placed in rows. As I would complete a task, into the trash bin it went. It is vital to come up with some sort of system to capture your thoughts or things people tell you, because the reality is, your memory is going to be sketchy at best. With the advent of smart phones, I'm sure there is an app for menopausal brain storage!

Effects on Driving

Crazy woman driver. Have you ever heard that phrase? Well, during menopause I learned the source of the saying and the truth of it. All of this pruning and reconfiguring can also interfere with your ability to drive and remember basic traffic laws. I remember one day sitting in the left turn lane and suddenly, after 30 years of driving, having absolutely no idea who had the right-of-way, the person turning left or the person turning right. Another day I drove right through a red light before the signal from my eyes reached my brain to explain to me that it was a red light. It took another few seconds for that signal to process and its meaning get interpreted. By that time I was all the way through the light (luckily, safely). I ran through stop signs and found myself suddenly confused by signs that used to seem so clear to me.

I have talked with several women about this curious loss of memory concerning traffic laws. Seems that a number of women have experienced the same area of confusion. I think it is a grace of God that the time in which you are going through menopause is the same time your kids are learning to drive. I was able to review all the traffic laws while teaching them to drive, and once they got their license, I allowed them to drive me as much as possible.

So my advice to you is to hire a chauffeur for the 10 years surrounding menopause if you can afford it, if not, be extra careful, take your time, and if anyone else offers to drive, take them up on it. Oh, and one more thing, the next time you see a crazy woman driver run the red light, instead of screaming angrily at her, simply smile, shake your head with compassion, and say knowingly, "Poor thing, she must be going through menopause."

Impaired Decision Making

Another side effect of this pruning process is the difficulty in making decisions and evaluating alternatives. I remember being at Bass Pro Shop looking at camping stoves trying to decide which one to buy for my husband for Christmas. There were only two choices but I seemed unable to decide which would be best. One came with a griddle and was a few dollars more than the other. After weighing the two options for about 5 minutes, my daughter said to my mother-in-law, "Come on, Grandma. Let's go look around. She will be here for a while." I was a little hurt by her comment but she turned out to be right. It took me 20 minutes to decide between the two. I left the store wondering what had happened to me. I used to be very skilled at making decisions and making them quickly. Had I changed so much that even my daughter had noticed my inability to make decisions? The answer is yes. After struggling for quite some time, I finally decided to allow my husband and children to make the decisions wherever possible. Take heart, as the hormonal storm in your brain subsides, your memory and decision-making abilities will return. And better yet, your decision-making ability will actually improve. The rewiring and hormonal changes light up the intuitive area of your brain making the post-menopausal woman much wiser. This is why older women are perceived to be wiser because, in actual fact, they are. This is also why the Bible charges the older women to train up the younger women. Not only do we have more life experience, but we are truly wiser.

Chapter 3
Changes in Your Emotions

The thing that is really hard, and really amazing,
is giving up on being perfect and beginning the
work of becoming yourself.
– Anna Quindlen

nother interesting aspect of the God ordained purpose behind our changing brains and hormones is the affect it has on our emotions. High estrogen levels give us great emotional strength and allow us to push down things that are bothering us or irritating us, but when estrogen decreases, we no longer have the emotional strength to keep things "shoved down." This is why many women get irritable and emotional around the beginning of their periods because estrogen drops dramatically right before your period starts.

Women who are emotionally healthy have less PMS symptoms than those of us who have a lot of emotional baggage. And while many of us can hold it together for the few days each month when our estrogen is low, during perimenopause, when our estrogen is low for weeks and months on end, we no longer have the emotional capital to keep it pushed down. Our loving heavenly Father desires nothing more than for His daughters to walk in peace and complete healing. He has given us approximately 500 report cards during our years of menstruation to try and get us to deal with our junk. Menopause is His last great effort to wake us up to what is going on inside of us, deal with our pasts, and implement much needed change. As our hormones fluctuate, God can use this time where we are weakened to bring up areas that need healing. If you will cooperate with the process, God will use it as a time of pruning and purging as He gets you ready for the next phase of your life. This part is no exception. God wants you to give birth to yourself, and as everyone woman knows, birth is a very messy business. For me, it was particularly messy.

My Quest for Understanding

She could never go back and make some of the
details pretty. All she could do was move forward
and make the whole beautiful.
− Terri St. Cloud

When I first began having all my health problems, the first question every doctor would ask was, "Are you under a lot of stress?" Whether it was the neurologist I consulted about migraines, the gastrologist for acid reflux, the cardiologist for irregular heartbeat, or the endocrinologist for fatigue, the question was the same, "Are you under a lot of stress?" and my response was always the same, "No, I'm not under any stress. My marriage is good, our finances are fine, and my children are great. There is nothing in my life that is stressful." But as I prayed for God to heal me, He showed me that although there was no external stress in my life, the amount of pressure I was putting on myself was destroying my health.

In my 20's and 30's I struggled with a lot of self-hate, self-rejection, unworthiness, perfectionism, guilt, and shame. I was constantly beating up on myself in my mind, criticizing myself, judging my performance and telling myself I needed to be doing more and doing it better. The world relentlessly promotes the image of the perfect home, perfect figure, perfect career, perfect parent, and perfect life. The false expectations I had placed on myself and was trying to live up to were literally killing me, slowly but surely, as the stress began to affect every area of my body. As I cried out to God to heal my body and seemed to get no response, God gave me a dream to show me what was hindering my physical healing.

I was at church and a woman was having a baby in the sanctuary. Several women were helping deliver the baby and after it came out, one woman wrapped it in a blanket and then began carrying the newborn around and showing it to everyone. Everyone at church was oohing and ahhing over the baby, but when it was my turn to see the baby, I was surprised and a little horrified to see just the head of the baby. There was no body, just the head, but it was smiling and cooing just like any other baby. I was very confused about how it could be alive without a body, but even more confused by the fact that no one else seemed to think this was strange. Eventually, I pulled one of the ladies of the church aside and asked her where the rest of the body was. She replied, "Oh that will be delivered later," like that's how it always happens.

What God showed me through this dream, was that my head had to be delivered before he could ever deliver my body. My mind was what was making me sick and so only through its healing could my body begin to heal. By cooperating with the Holy Spirit, and letting God heal all of the old wounds, repenting of my sins, letting go of bitterness and reconciling with people, was I able to begin healing.

I didn't understand what was happening to me or why I couldn't just "snap out of it." For a time, I thought that I had gotten off the path and began to seek the Lord for where I went wrong and how I was supposed to get back on track. But as I prayed and sought the Lord, I realized that I was on the path He had laid out for me. Although it was a dark path, He was with me and would carry me through. In some cases, the path doubled back and the Lord made me look squarely at the past, deal with the hurts and the regrets, see the past for what it really was, and where necessary, let it go. At other turns in the road, He took me to a high hill and allowed me glimpses of the road ahead. I cried and cried and often wanted to turn back, but He continued to lead me onward.

I used to think the Christian journey was a straight uphill road, but I have learned that it is quite different. It is a road fraught with pot holes, terrifying stretches with sheer cliffs on either side, wonderful segments through beautiful meadows, exhilarating moments standing on the heights and hairpin curves where you think you are doubling back over ground you have already covered. Although the menopausal years were one portion of the journey that I wished I could have skipped, I have come to appreciate them and even thank the Lord for that particular stretch of rugged terrain, for it is during the difficult parts of the journey where we seem to learn and grow the most.

Stress

Though my journey was particularly rocky, it doesn't have to be that way for everyone. Stress is a key contributor to how many symptoms you experience during menopause, as well as the magnitude of those symptoms. Managing stress, whether internal or external, is an important aspect in maintaining your health and easing the menopausal transition. Many of the symptoms associated with menopause are also associated with stress. Low estrogen effects your emotional strength and your ability to handle stress effectively.

I have often wondered why our mothers didn't seem to have as many symptoms and problems with menopause. Some of it has to do with the hormone replacements they took but I believe it also has to do with our corrupted food supply and the increased stress levels in our society. Due to the genetic engineering, modern farming methods/pesticides, and convenience foods, our food is less nutritious and filled with hormones and chemicals, which affect our bodies. Add to that the increased stress level we live under and it's no wonder we are having a harder time. The women of yester-year did not have to contend with emails, texts, or Facebook, nor did they have to contend with running children to a thousand different activities, volunteering, attending bible studies, and/or holding down careers. The pace of life we live in has never been experienced by any other generation. Our foremothers had hard lives of physical labor but their days weren't driven by the clock, frantically trying to get things done by a certain time. Their lives started early in the day, but had a gentle routine with no hard deadlines. They knew when to take a break, sit down with a glass of lemonade and just stare off into the distance. In the heat of the day, they would often come inside, sit down and sew or snap beans for dinner. I once read in an antique book on home management the suggestion that the lady of the house take a brief nap before her husband arrived home so she could be fresh and joyful when he arrived.

I don't know about you, but I find it nearly impossible to sit down for a break knowing the thousand and one things still left to be done. My days often feel rushed and it is as if an invisible hand is pushing me through my day, nudging me to go faster and do more. Our larger homes, filled with lots of things, are beautiful, but they require more time and energy to maintain than the 1,000 square foot homes of our parents and grandparents.

Is it any wonder that many of the symptoms of menopause are also stress related? Take a look at this list of symptoms for stress:

Emotional symptoms of stress include
- Becoming easily agitated, frustrated, and moody
- Feeling overwhelmed, like you are losing control or need to take control
- Having difficulty relaxing and quieting your mind
- Feeling bad about yourself (low self-esteem), lonely, worthless, and depressed
- Avoiding others

Physical symptoms of stress include
- Low energy
- Headaches
- Upset stomach, including diarrhea, constipation, and nausea
- Aches, pains, and tense muscles
- Chest pain and rapid heartbeat
- Insomnia
- Frequent colds and infections
- Loss of sexual desire and/or ability

- Nervousness and shaking, ringing in the ear, cold or sweaty hands and feet
- Dry mouth and difficulty swallowing
- Clenched jaw and grinding teeth

Cognitive symptoms of stress include
- Constant worrying
- Racing thoughts
- Forgetfulness and disorganization
- Inability to focus
- Poor judgment
- Being pessimistic or seeing only the negative side

Behavioral symptoms of stress include
- Changes in appetite—either not eating or eating too much
- Procrastinating and avoiding responsibilities
- Increased use of alcohol, drugs, or cigarettes
- Exhibiting more nervous behaviors, such as nail biting, fidgeting, and pacing

Do you notice the similarities between this list and the list of menopausal symptoms? Stress affects every aspect of your body, including your emotions, behaviors, attitudes, mental abilities, and physical health. No system or part of your body is immune. Take time to look at your life, your commitments and your mental and emotional health and see if there are any areas of stress. Then, seek the Lord for ways to remove some of those stressors from your life and get professional help if you need it. Your life and health depend on it.

Joyce Meyer in her book *Eat the Cookie...Buy the Shoes: Giving Yourself Permission to Lighten Up*, gives this suggestion for combating stress, "My suggestion to avoid bitterness, resentment, and perhaps a mild nervous breakdown is to take time between the spring cleaning and all the rest of the things on your schedule and do something that you really enjoy that would qualify as celebration. The first thing your mind is going to say is, "You don't have time to do that." But I am telling you that you need to take the time. And if you do, the rest of your tasks will go more smoothly and joyfully. If you don't take the time to recharge your batteries, then you are probably headed for some version of sinking emotions—discouragement, depression, despair, anger, resentment, or self-pity. When you start to feel down, just take the time to do something "up" that lifts your mood and helps you feel better about life in general."

Adopting an attitude of celebration can make the most mundane day fun and uplifting. Get creative. Celebrating can be as simple as giving yourself an imaginary high-five or throwing your arms up in the air, jogging in place, and yelling wahoo as if you have just crossed the finish line of the Boston Marathon. Celebrating can take the form of a cup of tea or a piece of chocolate. It doesn't have to be expensive or time consuming. Remember it is a life style and an attitude. Celebrating lifts our spirits, encourages us and changes the atmosphere for everyone around us. Give it a try.

No Such Place as Done

Come to me, all who labor and are heavy laden,
and I will give you rest. Take my yoke upon you,
and learn from me, for I am gentle and lowly in
heart, and you will find rest for your souls. For my
yoke is easy, and my burden is light.
− Matthew 11:28-29
Busyness is an illness of the spirit.
− Eugene Peterson

For several years I struggled mightily with feelings of being overwhelmed and inadequate. I would write down my to-do list in the morning, and at the end of the day fall into bed exhausted and demoralized, beating myself up mentally for not getting "anything" done that day. I was frustrated, confused, and angry and upset with myself. How could the whole day go by and I get absolutely nothing accomplished, I would ask myself. This happened most every evening, each day ending the same way, exhausted and defeated.

One morning I was journaling with the Lord and laying my complaint before Him. "Lord, why can't I get anything done? What's the matter with me?" The Lord gently replied, "Vicki, there is no such place as Done. You have a false expectation that at the end of the day EVERYTHING should be done. That's an impossibility. Even if you were able to actually get to a place where everything was done — all the laundry was clean, overhead light fixtures clean, baseboards washed, cabinets clean and organized, mending completed, all emails responded to and taken care of, every weed pulled, lesson plans ready to go, and all your friends called and caught up with, it wouldn't last more than 8 hours at most. By the time you woke up in the morning, there would be clothes to wash, breakfast to make, dishes to clean, emails to respond to, and school to teach.

Thinking that you can get to a place where you can sit down, look around, and have absolutely nothing to do, is a false expectation. You'll never get there. Each day has its own list of things that need to be accomplished and there will always be things left for tomorrow. The key is simply taking each day and doing the things required for that day. When you lie down at night and complain that you got nothing done, that's a lie. You cooked three meals, homeschooled your children, took them to piano lessons, replied to emails, made necessary phone calls, did some cleaning, fed the dog, spent time with your husband and kids, cleaned dishes, and many other tasks. If you didn't get to the things on your to-do list, it is because, in reality, they didn't need to get done that day. You did the things that needed to get done. You were faithful with what you were given. Don't worry about the tasks on the list. They will get done when the time is right. Come to me all you who are weary and are heavy burdened and learn from me, for my yoke is easy and my burden is light. Each day you are carrying a month's worth of tasks to do rather than simply addressing the needs of the day. Learn to accept that there are things still to be done. There always will be. Let them rest in my arms and I will show you when they need to be done. Allow me to schedule your day and your tomorrows, and everything will get done in its proper time."

This was such a revelation for me. It seems obvious now, but when I was in the midst of it, I couldn't see how unrealistic I was. Slowly but surely I learned to seek the Lord for what He wanted to accomplish for the day and to leave the rest in His capable hands. Believe it or not, the lawn was not overtaken with weeds, the mending got done, no one went without clean clothes, and the house did not fall apart. I even began to learn how to rest.

Learning to Rest

Stand by the roads, and look, and ask for the
ancient paths, where the good way is; and walk in
it, and find rest for your souls.
– Jeremiah 6:16

As a culture, we have become obsessed with productivity. It is a society that says, "Go, go, go." Our forefathers and mothers knew the wisdom of times of rest. Their days had a simple rhythm of work hard, take a break, work hard, and take a break. I can remember helping my grandmother with a task and after an hour or two of working, she would say, "Well, Vicki, I think it's time for a glass of iced tea." We would pour ourselves some tea and then sit on the porch and listen to the birds sing or sit in the recliners in the living room and rock for 20 minutes. After our break, she would say, "Well, let's get back to work." Lunch was never rushed but used as a time to relax and rest. I don't remember ever working more than two hours before we would stop for a break. Those little breaks made the day and the task more enjoyable. I loved helping my grandmother and the pleasant companionship of just sitting together quietly enjoying the pleasure of resting or chatting about nothing in particular.

Somehow, over the years, I lost the lesson of rest my grandmother taught me. I became driven; constantly feeling rushed and pressured to get things accomplished. I honestly could not sit down for five minutes to rest without feeling guilty that I was wasting time. If I laid down for a much needed nap, I scolded myself for the time I had wasted. The inability to rest only exacerbated my fatigue and increased my stress levels.

God ordained rest into creation and it was the first thing He instituted. After creating man, He rested. God established a day of rest each week, periodic festivals for rest (some lasting an entire week), and a yearlong rest from planting and reaping. And, in the year of Jubilee, the rest period was two years. So if God ordained and consecrated rest, why is it that we struggle to rest? If you ask ten people if they feel more acceptable when they are working or resting, all ten will respond when they are working. Our society has become obsessed with productivity, but the irony is that if we take time to rest we will actually be more productive. Joyce Meyer suggests that we call even small moments of rest "vacations." When we say the word vacation a restful spirit seems to come over us. Give this a try: The next time you sit down for a few minutes to drink your ice tea and someone asks you what you are doing, simply smile and reply, "I'm taking a ten minute vacation" and really enjoy your vacation from work.

Since I read Joyce's suggestion, I have noticed that I rarely use the term vacation. I might say I'm going away for the weekend, or taking a trip, or visiting family. I rarely say I'm going on vacation. Somehow I feel the need to mask the fact that I am going somewhere to rest. The other phrases seem to imply I am going somewhere to accomplish some purpose. My husband, in contrast, will repeat the phrase, "I'm on vacation" starting the moment he leaves work and then repeats it at least once a day for the duration of his vacation, celebrating and reminding himself to fully embrace the wonderful feeling of being on vacation.

Rest is something we can learn to do. It is an attitude we can develop and a lifestyle we can choose. Learning to rest will ease the journey through menopause by decreasing your stress levels and make it much more enjoyable.

Grief

I spent the summer of my 48th year on the verge of tears. I didn't know why I felt like crying, but the tears were always just under the surface ready to spring out at the slightest provocation and sometimes with no provocation at all. I spent the summer asking myself, *What's the matter with me? Is this hormonal?* I told myself to get over it. I spent months in frustration over this seemingly incomprehensible desire to cry.

One day a friend called and innocently asked, "How are you?" The next thing I knew I was telling her I was a wreck and didn't know what was wrong with me. I concluded the conversation by blurting out, "I think I need to see a counselor." I was shocked by the comment but knew it was true. After I hung up the phone, I called a Christian counselor to make an appointment. The Lord knew what I needed, and someone had just canceled. I was able to go straight over to her office. As I began to meet with her, it quickly became apparent to her that I was grieving.

Grieving?...Grieving What? As we explored my feelings, I found I was grieving on multiple levels and over multiple losses. My mother had died at the age of 49 and as I approached my 49th birthday, I was thinking a lot about my mom which triggered a new stage of grief.

My daughter was getting ready to enter the eleventh grade and the college process would soon get underway in earnest. As we began talking about which colleges she wanted to visit in the fall, the reality she would soon be leaving home began to set in. With my son only two years behind her, the realization that my parenting years were drawing to a close brought a deep sadness and sense of loss. My children were no longer little and the days of homeschooling and being together all day were almost gone. I didn't want it to end. I loved our time together, and so as I contemplated the end of this season of my life, I grieved.

Not all of my grief was quite so tangible. I had to recognize the loss of some dreams and expectations that would never be—the "if only's." I had high hopes of doing certain things with my kids that I had never gotten around to, and I had visions of being the perfect super mom. I had to face the reality that my children were too old for those activities now, and we would never get to go back and do them. As I worked through my grief and let go of the past, God enabled me to accept the mom I was rather than the mom I had hoped to be. Christiane Northrup in *The Wisdom of Menopause* says, "The second requirement for transformation is more difficult by far: we must be willing to feel the pain of loss and grieve for those parts of our lives that we are leaving behind. And that includes our fantasies of how our lives could have been different if only. Facing up to such loss is rarely easy, and that is why so many of us resist change in general and at midlife in particular."

Along with these impending changes was the need to face the already present changes in my physical body. Though we are aging and changing every day of our lives, during the years of puberty and the years surrounding menopause, the changes to our physical appearance seem to go into hyper-drive. It seemed like overnight that the face staring me back in the mirror had aged 10 years. My hair turned gray, lines appeared around my eyes and mouth. Age spots appeared all over my skin from head to toe. My breasts began a slow descent down my chest, my upper arms began to jiggle no matter how much I exercised, and my stomach and hips had a new layer of padding on them that refused to come off. The face in the mirror actually looked like one of those "older women."

What happened to the cute young slender thing I used to be? I would gaze longingly at dress styles I used to look great in and cry because I knew I could no longer wear them. They didn't look good on my new, more mature figure. I didn't want these changes. I didn't want to grow old. It may sound silly, but I grieved over not being able to wear the style of clothes I once wore. I would walk into a store, see a really cute dress and then realize the dress was not appropriate for my figure or my age. I would stand in front of the mirror and realize I looked like a fifty-year-old woman trying to look like a twenty-year-old. A sadness would come over me, as if I had lost something and I cried. I found I had to shop at new stores. I remember the day I took my sister, who is seven years younger than me, to my new favorite stores only to have her gently tell me that these styles were too old for her. I cried again. Though we all know we will grow older, I had never stopped to think about how the changes would make me feel.

I share this not to depress you but to prepare you for the range of emotions you will experience. Much like how my daughter cried during puberty because she didn't want to change and grow up, we don't want to change either. She didn't want to have to shave her legs and wash her face twice a day, nor did she like getting acne or having to wear deodorant. She was quite happy the way she was! But growing up brings transitions, and we never finish growing up. Menopause is just another stage in our growing up process, and like my daughter, we will blossom into something new and beautiful. Anais Nin wrote, "Then the time came when the risk it took to remain tight in a bud was more painful than the risk it took to blossom." Menopause is our time to blossom. Take the risk, leave behind what needs to be left behind, and embrace what is yet to come.

As we move through the grieving process, acceptance of the losses in our lives comes in stages. Menopause usually occurs during the years when our children are leaving the nest, our parents are aging and our role in their lives is changing. Our forties and fifties are years filled with a great deal of transitions and therefore losses. Holly Shut, in *Midlife Momentum*, puts it this way, "There is no denying that we continually face change, and all change involves loss. However, as we continue to age beyond fifty these changes and losses roll up onto our shores like waves intensifying in a storm. We need skills and perspective to navigate these swells of loss in healthy, depth-enriching ways."

So grieve what is lost, cry and maybe cry a little more, then take your tissues, dry your eyes and embrace the joy and beauty of this next stage of life. Yes, beauty, the beauty that radiates from within as we come into a place of peace, joy, and contentment that is forged through the process of menopause. As we face our losses and embrace the process of letting go, we begin to see all of the possibilities of this new season: the extra free time we will have now that the responsibility of raising our children is waning, the pleasure of reconnecting with our husbands and the excitement we had in the early days of our marriage as we have more time to play together and more energy for each other, and the freedom to travel and spend time in creative pursuits. A whole new life is opening up. What would you like to accomplish in this next season?

My desire for you is to navigate this time of transition by fully feeling what you feel, but also by embracing what is yet to come. If you feel sad, then grieve, but don't stay there. Healthy grieving ends up in hope for the future. Unhealthy grieving ends up in self-pity, bitterness, and regret. If you need help with your grief, then please seek help from a counselor, pastor, or friend. Just as you would not wish for your daughter to stay a child forever because you know of the wonderful experiences that can only be experienced by growing up, so too, God does not want us to stay young women forever because there are many wonderful experiences and adventures that cannot be experienced until we reach this new stage. Embrace the possibilities that these losses open up and dare to start dreaming.

To grant to those who grieve in Zion—
to bestow on them a crown of beauty instead of
ashes,
the oil of joy instead of mourning,
and a garment of praise instead of a spirit of
heaviness.
They will be called oaks of righteousness,
a planting of the Lord for the display of his
splendour.
– Isaiah 61:3

A Time for Reflection

- Do you feel a sense of loss in any area(s) of your life?
- Are there any positives or new possibilities associated with these losses?
- If you have children, what will you do when your evening and weekends are no longer consumed with your children's activities?
- What have you always longed to do if you had the time?

Learning to Laugh

The journey through menopause can be difficult, frustrating and downright depressing at times. That's why it is important to lighten up. One of the most valuable weapons we have to combat the emotional and physical havoc of menopause and ease the transition is laughter. Learning to laugh at ourselves will go a long way towards improving our overall mood and health. Laughter releases feel-good hormones, endorphins, which produce physical, mental and social benefits.

Physical Benefits
- Boosts the immune system
- Decreases pain by producing natural pain killers
- Improves sleep
- Lowers blood pressure
- Lowers stress hormones such as cortisol and adrenaline
- Relaxes the muscles
- Prevents heart disease
- Stimulates blood circulation and oxygenation

Mental Benefits
- Aids in relaxation
- Increases memory, creativity, alertness and learning
- Reduces stress
- Improves mood and increases joy
- Lessens anxiety and depression
- Shifts perspective about situations

Social Benefits
- Strengthens relationships
- Helps connect people

- Increases personal satisfaction
- Increase ability to cope with difficult situations
- Diffuses tension during conflict
- Heals rifts and eases forgiveness
- Decreases defensiveness
- Encourages spontaneity
- Draws others to us

There was a time during menopause when I realized that I hadn't laughed in years. Maybe a brief chuckle here and there but I hadn't had a good belly laugh since I couldn't remember when. My husband and children laughed, but for some reason it had become difficult for me to join in their fun. I had become so serious and depressed that I had forgotten the importance of lightening up and laughing. I asked Jesus to teach me to laugh again.

Researchers determined that adults laugh approximately 25 times a day and children laugh, on average, 400 times a day! I don't know about you, but I rarely laugh 25 times a day, but I am committed to learning to laugh more. Even if you have to force yourself to laugh in the beginning, it will get easier and easier until it becomes a lifestyle. It is hard to be angry, depressed, or frustrated when you are laughing.

Make it a mission to discover ways to incorporate humor into your life and get your family involved. I started by buying a 365 day calendar with a cartoon for every day. My husband and I started watching funny shows in the evening to dissipate any negativity or tension from the day. You can also check out joke books from the library and read a few jokes each day or spend time around people who make you laugh. Find children to play with and laugh when they laugh. But most importantly, the next time you do something crazy or can't remember where the car keys are, instead of getting upset and crying, stop and laugh. You will find that your days go more smoothly, your family will stop avoiding you, and your menopause symptoms will decrease.

My friends and I used to share our menopausal moments so we could laugh about them together. It created a great sense of camaraderie as we went through the process. My friend, Christine, once shared that after going to the post office and dropping off some letters, she went to the library to return some books, but upon her arrival, she discovered her letters still sitting on the seat. Yes, she had put her library books in the mailbox. She had to return to the post office and ask if they would open the mailbox so she could retrieve her library books. The post office reassured her that she wasn't the first.

Things are going to happen, so just learn to laugh. I'll leave you with these words of wisdom from Ecclesiastes 8:15, "So I commend the enjoyment of life, because there is nothing better for a person under the sun than to eat and drink and be glad. Then joy will accompany them in their toil all the days of the life God has given them under the sun."

Part 2
Is There Life After Menopause?

Chapter 4
Divine Plan

Our vision of God always requires an upgrade to enable us to see who we are going to become in the next season.
— Graham Cooke

ne of my favorite quotes from Pamela Smith's *Take Charge of the Change* says,

"Other cultures have a greatly different attitude towards menopause than our own. In some cultures it is seen as a positive change —freedom from the need for contraception and from the ups and downs of the monthly period, and the arrival of a new status of "wise woman.... I believe that we were created for the change—it is a divinely designed natural life process—and perimenopause is a natural crossing through it. I don't believe that it's a dirty trick played on women, as a life sentence, nor a sickness to be tolerated. I believe that, similar to puberty and pregnancy, there is a master plan and purpose genetically scripted into every cell of the female

body to orchestrate and direct the transformation we call menopause."

As you navigate the journey through menopause, much of the journey can be depressing and discouraging. Some days you feel so tired you don't think you can get out of bed. Other days, you are discouraged because you feel as if you haven't accomplished anything. On still others, you want to cry because of what you see in the mirror or read on the scales. Though there are many negatives on this journey, we have a choice. We can either focus on the negatives or choose to focus on the positives and the amazing design of God's plan. We can choose to see and celebrate the small accomplishments and miracles of each day. Learning to celebrate can be a key antidote to all the negative changes taking place and focus on the positive ones. Most of our days are made up of the ordinary, and so we think there is nothing to celebrate, but getting the house cleaned or finishing a load of laundry is an accomplishment we can celebrate.

God's ultimate goal is to transform us into the likeness of His Son that we might be able to receive His love and return His love. Menopause is His last great push to birth us into the inheritance we were destined for before the world began. In our younger years we were distracted and worried about looks, status, and prestige. We tended to be self-focused and consumed with our own lives. As we journeyed through life, we picked up wounds, disappointments, false expectations and lies along the way. Jesus uses our hormones to remove the veil we've been hiding behind and tear down the walls we have built so we can take an honest look inside. Jesus wants us to use this time of menopause to press the "pause" button and spend time in reflection. As we open our hearts to Him, He takes us through an incredible process of discovery and healing, as He walks us to the top of this mountain where we can see the

Promised Land. Much like the Israelites had to spend 40 years in the desert in order to be prepared to enter the Promise Land; God has been preparing us to enter our promised land. And just like the Israelites that left Egypt had to die in the desert and only their offspring were allowed to enter the Promised Land, so to our self must be left behind so the women we are giving birth to can enter the Promised Land.

Most women find this new stage of life deeply satisfying. Christiane Northrup states, "A 1998 Gallup survey, presented at the annual meeting of the North American Menopause Society, showed that more than half of American women between the ages of fifty and sixty-five felt happiest and most fulfilled a this stage of life. Compared to when they were in their twenties, thirties, and forties, they felt their lives had improved in many ways, including family life, interests, friendships, and their relationship with their spouse. In other words, the conventional view of menopause as a scary transition heralding "the beginning of the end" couldn't be further from the truth." All the hormonal changes, the brain rewiring, the physical, mental and emotional changes are designed by a loving Father to set His daughters free. There is no room in your next stage for bitterness and regrets. Maybe that's why it's called the golden years. If you will cooperate with God's plan and allow Him to transform not only your body but also your mind and emotions, you will emerge ready and able to fulfill your purpose and calling.

Chapter 5
Changing Identity

*There are pressures in our younger years and first
adulthood that strip us of who we truly are. Midlife
can be that time of coming home to who we are
created to be, launching us into a life of confidence,
joy and purpose.*
– Holly Shut, Midlife Momentum.

For several years I looked forward to the empty nest. Freedom from the responsibilities of day-to-day parenting, children's activities, and homeschooling was at times intoxicating. I wanted to toss it aside and run blissfully into a life with free time, date nights, friends, traveling, and walking around in my underwear. I was excited about the possibilities for my marriage, my friendships, and my future employment. But now that I am one year out, I find that excitement is receding and the grief and uncertainty returning.

For those of you who worked outside the home during your parenting years, this transition may not be as stark, nor may you face the identity crisis that comes to the moms who stayed at home, and especially to the moms who homeschooled their children. I remember the identity crisis I went through when I left the workplace and became a stay-at-home mom. I had enjoyed my work and found great fulfillment in it. When people asked me what I did for a living, I was proud to tell them I was an electrical engineer working for a software company as a manager. I remember the first time someone asked me what I did after I quit and my only answer was that I stayed home with the baby. I also remember the first time I had to fill out the form at the doctor's office and fill in the blank for "occupation." What do I write? What do I put down? It took several years and different wording until I settled on homemaker. The first few months of being home was lonely as all my friends were at work. I struggled with feelings of incompetence, as I had no idea how to take care of a baby. I had been a successful businesswoman managing 10 people and multiple projects, and now I couldn't even manage one baby and get the laundry done.

It never occurred to me that my changing identity would be so difficult. As the years went by, I embraced my new identity and loved being a homemaker and homeschool mom. What a surprise it has been to find myself struggling once again with my changing identity in the reverse. Who will I be once the kids are gone? What will I do with my life and my time? Will I be able to re-enter the workforce and compete against people with 30 years of work experience? Will employers value the "work" I have done for the last 20 years? I find that there is a certain loneliness as my remaining child drives himself everywhere he needs to go. No longer do I see my homeschool friends at all our different functions. They no longer come over for playdates where we get to sit and talk while the children play. Just as my work friends slowly drifted away because our lives were going in different directions and we no longer saw each other on a daily basis, so now, my "mom" friends are drifting away as our lives move off in different directions.

This has been a time of uncertainty and confusion mixed with the grief of what is passing away. I don't want it to end. I don't want things to change. But life goes on, we visit colleges, we prepare. I just didn't expcct to struggle. I knew I would grieve, but I was unprepared for the feelings of being adrift. The best way I have to explain it is to say it feels like I am in a vast ocean. The sun is directly overhead, and there is no way of knowing which direction I am going, but I know that I am in a current that is taking me where I need to go.

Some days I am content to trust that God will get me where I need to go, but then the consuming desire to know where I am headed overtakes me and I begin to worry and stress about what I am going to do next year. Should I be doing something to prepare? Should I get a part-time job? Go back to school? And yet, I want to savor every possible moment I have left with my son before this part of the journey is over. Up, down, and all around my emotions go, never staying the same. I am in the midst of a great transition.

This is a season for savoring the blessing of being home, of time with my children and time with the Lord. It is a season for pondering who I am, what I enjoy, what I am passionate about, where I want to go, and what I want to do with my life. It is also a season of rest. The demands of parenting have lessened, and I no longer actively teach my son. It has been so long since I had space in my schedule that I find it disconcerting. What do you do with free time? But most importantly, it is a season of becoming.

Chapter 6
Changing Roles – Men and Women

Grow old along with me! The best is yet to be...
– Robert Browning

ave you ever wondered why so many couples divorce in their 40's and 50's? Many people attribute it to the fact that couples have been focused on their kids for so long, they no longer have anything in common. While this may be part of the cause, I think the bigger cause stems from the fact that both partners are being completely transformed, and if they don't understand the changes that are taking place, see the beauty in the changes and embrace them together, they will wind up drifting apart missing the richness of the new relationship they could have had.

The years surrounding midlife are a time of great transition, not only for you, but also for your husband. We often hear about men's "mid-life crisis," but women go through their own crisis as well. Do you remember how you struggled during the years of puberty between wanting to be a little girl and play with your dolls and then in the next moment, wanting to put on makeup and be noticed by the boys? Do you remember the hardships this placed on your friendships as some of you progressed faster than others? Perhaps your best friend still wanted to play house but you no longer had any desire to play those childhood games. You had moved on to a new stage. Many friendships dissolved during the turbulent junior high school years, sometimes to be renewed in high school, sometimes not.

The same thing is occurring during the time of menopause and a man's mid-life crisis. Our hormones are completely changing us and with those changes, our desires are changing as well. One day we want to go back to being that "cute young thing" that was carefree, wore bikinis, and was free to come and go as she pleased. The next day, we are so glad we are not that person anymore and enjoy the peace and content of our new stage of life. While you are struggling between the old you and the new, your husband is dealing with similar changes. One day he wants to buy a motorcycle and the next day a La-Z-Boy© recliner!

And not only are we struggling to move on from who we were to whom we are becoming, but our whole focus in life and our priorities are shifting as well. I found this to be one of the most fascinating aspects of the transformation taking place.

When we go through puberty, the hormone estrogen increases and triggers our reproductive system to kick into gear. For men, the hormone testosterone increases, kicking their reproductive system into overdrive. When we are in the childbearing years, our increased estrogen stimulates the part of the brain that makes us want to nurture and focus on the needs of other people. During these years, we are focused homeward and want to nest and have children. While at this same time, high estrogen dampens the creative portion of our brains and the portion that wants to make a difference in the world. As our estrogen begins to decrease in our 40's and 50's we suddenly begin to shift from an inward focus to an outward one, focusing more on the world around us. We lose interest in cooking for the family and taking care of the house. We become restless and gifts and desires that have long remained dormant begin to surface. We become more creative and have an urge to change the world around us. We find ourselves wanting to go back to work or get involved with a ministry and have an impact on the world. As estrogen decreases, our creativity starts to blossom and to our surprise, we discover hidden creative talents. Do you remember Grandma Moses? She began painting in 1936 at the age of 76. Two years later her paintings were discovered by an art collector and she became a renowned artist. Menopause is a very exciting time as new ideas and passions begin to emerge and new possibilities begin to open up on the horizon.

At the exact same time that your focus is shifting from homeward to the world, your husband's is shifting from the world, homeward. As his testosterone decreases, his drive to conquer the world begins to wane and he begins to turn homeward. He is ready to retire, buy some woodworking tools and stay around the house and putter.

As you can imagine, these shifts can cause a lot of conflict in a marriage. As the wife wants to go out and do things, the husband wants to stay home. Add to that, the internal conflict to fulfill her duties at home while everything inside is screaming to be about the business of the world. We must take care to acknowledge these feelings and desires while at the same time not abdicate our responsibilities at home. The wise woman will use these transition years to nurture these new desires and prepare for her future while at the same time taking care of her home. I have seen too many women completely abandon their responsibilities at home by taking on jobs that take them away from home 5 days a week, or going back to school fulltime to the point that the demands of school don't allow them to be home with their families. One woman I know took off to China to teach English as a foreign language, completely leaving her family for 9 months out of the year. I'm not saying you can't have a full-time job or go back to school. Many women do this very successfully while raising a family. I'm just cautioning you to check your motivations and do it in a balanced way. It's imperative that we understand the changes taking place inside us. If the husband doesn't understand the changes taking place, he can become angry and feel like his wife doesn't care about him, their children, or their home any more. The wife feels like he doesn't support her dreams and is holding her back. You can see how these misunderstandings and conflicts can lead to divorce. Talk with your husband about the new feelings and longings stirring up inside of you. Work out a plan to begin nurturing these desires in a balanced and responsible way.

During my own time of transition, I took on more responsibilities at church, took classes on inner healing, leadership, and drawing and started a part-time job. My children were in high school and required less hands-on teaching, were able to be left at home by themselves, and were able to help with more and more chores around the house. This allowed me more free time to pursue the things that interested me while still fulfilling my responsibilities at home. Though my desire to move into new areas was strong, I had to realize that the days with my children were quickly coming to a close and when they were gone, I would be free to pursue whatever interested me. God does not call us to abdicate our responsibilities. He calls us to be faithful to the ones He has given us. Our time will soon arrive, so be patient and use these years constructively. I've seen too much destruction in marriages and families during the midlife years. That is why I am so passionate about sharing this information with women around the world. My dear sisters, your marriage can withstand the inherent turmoil of this time of transition, but it takes understanding and communication.

There is beauty and purpose in God's design. When you were young and are having a family, God dampens the part of your brain that wants to conquer the world and enhances the nurturing area of your brains. At the same time, God increases men's testosterone while they are young and strong so they will work hard and provide for the family, fight the wars that need to be fought, and build what needs to be built.

But when the kids are grown, God unleashes His daughters who are now full of wisdom to solve the problems of the world. In days gone by, as women's physical bodies weakened and they could no longer help in the fields, and do all the physical labor required around the home, God in His infinite wisdom increased their creativity so they could create the things needed for the home. That's why we think of old women as quilting and knitting. By the same token, as the men's physical bodies weakened, they stayed at home focusing on the woodworking and other skills that were required to keep a homestead functioning. That's why we have an image of old men sitting around whittling. They were whittling new hoe handles, repairing harnesses, and making furniture. Each person in the family had their roles and the generations lived together, the younger members doing the physical labor and the older ones doing the creative tasks. God has designed our bodies to change with the different seasons of life so we are perfectly suited for each stage.

We live in a unique generation. The average life expectancy for women in 1900 was 48 years old. It wasn't until after 1950 that a woman could expect to live past 70. Average life expectancies for women are now into the 80's. Few of our great-grandmothers ever made it past menopause, if they were able to experience it at all, and for our grandmothers, menopause signaled a time of decline with only a few years remaining. For us and our mothers, we are the first generations to have a second adulthood. From the time we reach menopause and our children leave the home, we can expect approximately 30 years of good health and active living. When our grandparents thought about retirement, they knew they only had a few years left so they relaxed and spent time with family. For us however, spending thirty years playing golf and relaxing is an enormous waste of talents, abilities and energy. As we contemplate our retirement, let's enter it with purpose and with passion. Did you always want to be a doctor? There is no reason you shouldn't pursue it now. From age 20 to age 50 is a 30 year time span. We think nothing of going to college for four to eight years and then working for twenty-five years in a career, so what is to stop us now, when we have those same thirty years available to us, from pursuing anything we are passionate about?

I was talking with my friend Sandra the other day and she was sharing about how exciting this stage of life was for her and her husband. She said they have enjoyed dreaming about what they want to do after the kids are gone. They have decided to leave their large home and fix up an old homestead and start farming. She said her husband bought an old truck and said he couldn't begin to explain how great he felt driving around in that old truck. As we enter these turbulent waters of transition, we need to give each other the freedom to explore different identities and dreams. God has endowed you with gifts and abilities as well as experiences, wisdom and knowledge. What is He putting on your heart to do with your second adulthood? What are you passionate about? What have you always longed to do? Midlife is a time for dreaming and exploring new possibilities as the future opens up. Keep the lines of communication open and talk about the changes taking place. Share the dreams and desires each of you have for your futures. If he wants to take up woodworking, buy him some tools and be his biggest cheerleader. Does he suddenly want to grow his hair long? Let him try it out. Do you want to take up gardening? Go for it. Adopt an attitude of exploration and dreaming. Invest in each other's dreams.

A Time for Reflection

- Have you noticed these changing desires within yourself?
- What are your dreams and desires for the next season of your life?
- What can you be doing now to prepare for this next stage? Go back to school, get a part-time job, or take a short-term mission trip?

Action Steps

- Plan a weekend away with your spouse to talk about the future and how these changes are affecting your marriage.
- Renegotiate the responsibilities at home.
- Find out how you can support his dreams and desires for the future and communicate your needs to him.

Chapter 7
Glimpses from the Other Side

I thought that my midlife season would be about
pushing into a new future...and it is. I thought it
would be about leaving behind the expectations
and encumbrances of the past. It is. What I didn't
know is that it would feel so much like recovering
an essential self, not like discovering a new one.
– Shuana Niequist, Present Over Perfect
When we are who we are called to be, we will set
the world ablaze.
– St. Catherine of Sienat

From time to time I get glimpses of the other side, the side of the woman I am becoming. She is wise, peaceful, and full of grace and confidence. Her need to prove herself has waned as she knows who she is and whose she is. The wells of her creativity are returning and bursting forth in such a myriad of ways that she can't explore them all as quickly as she likes. She walks about with a new sense of freedom. Freedom to be the woman she was created to be. Free to laugh and be silly, free to rest and be quiet. Free to run and dance and twirl and skip. Free to meander and allow the days to unfold, resting in the knowledge that she is guided by an internal force who has her best interest at heart, a force that is always going ahead of her preparing the way. When the rough spots come, she rests in the knowledge that the Holy Spirit is going through it with her and there is a new aspect of the Father He wants to reveal and a new area He wants to transform.

She is able to cherish the uniqueness of each person even as she learns to treasure her own uniqueness. This woman I am becoming is renewing friendships, recovering relationships I thought were lost, and deepening those that have been idle or stagnant for many years.

Oh, sweet sisters, the journey may be long and arduous at times, but oh, the joy when it is complete. The scriptures say that Jesus, "for the joy set before him endured the cross." There is great joy and freedom on the other side of this transition. Look for it, search for it, it is there waiting to be discovered. The woman you always wanted to be is there waiting to emerge with passion and purpose much like a butterfly.

The butterfly begins its life as a caterpillar and then enters its cocoon to undergo a great transition. The interesting thing is that the caterpillar doesn't *do* anything while it is in the cocoon. It remains completely still and hemmed in, yet a great transformation is taking place. Every part of its body is affected, rewired, and reconfigured, until what emerges is barely recognizable to the caterpillar that went in. And yet, it is more beautiful and glorious, and can go higher and further than the caterpillar ever dreamed of going. The caterpillar was confined to the ground and limited in the range and scope of its travels, focused on getting through each day, and the things that sustain life: eating, sleeping, etc. The butterfly, however, is now free to explore just for the fun of exploring. It is free to rest and admire the beauty of the flowers or flit from place to place as its heart desires.

This is a glorious time of life. Allow God to have His way with you, even as the caterpillar allows Him to have His way with it. The process of emerging will be a struggle, yes, but the very struggle is what pumps blood into our wings so we can soar. We often want God to cut open the cocoon and free us quickly, but if we try and bypass the struggle, then we will end up crippled, holding on to the things of the past, unable to let go of the things that bound us and hindered us. Many women cut themselves free from spouses thinking this will alleviate the struggle and bring instant happiness and relief, but what they find is that they end up crippled and stunted. Work through the struggles and see where they can take you, how they can transform you, always keeping your eyes on the joy set before you. Freed from your responsibilities of raising a family, you are now free now to go where you wish and become the woman you were destined to be.

Recommended Reading

- *Take Charge of the Change*, Pamela M. Smith – Good in-depth discussion of menopause from a Biblical perspective. Includes lots of helpful tips for dealing with symptoms and living a healthy lifestyle.

- *The Wisdom of Menopause*, Christiane Northrup, M.D. – Comprehensive discussion of menopause. Best discussion on changes to the brain and emotions I have found anywhere. Caution: She speaks from a New Age perspective.

- *The Mermaid Chair*, Sue Monk Kidd – Fictional story of a woman going through a midlife crisis and the desire to throw off all responsibilities.

- *Midlife Momentum*, Holly Shut – Great book to help you find your purpose for your second adulthood.

- *Present Over Perfect: Leaving Behind Frantic For a Simpler, More Soulful Way of Living*, Shauna Niequist – If you struggle with perfectionism and feeling overwhelmed by too many commitments, this is a great book.

- *The Gifts of Imperfection*, Brene' Brown – Learn to let go of who you think you are supposed to be and embrace who you are.

- *Captivating*, John and Stasi Eldredge – Wonderful book about a woman's heart and the true nature of beauty. Every woman should read this.

- *Wild at Heart*, John Eldredge – Companion book to *Captivating* and teaches about a man's heart. If you are married or have a son, this book will give you a new understanding of their deepest needs.

Made in the USA
Monee, IL
19 January 2020